Irish Football Clubs in Liverpool

Why there were no Liverpool Celtics or Everton Hibernians

By David Kennedy and Peter Kennedy

Preface

Previously the impact of ethnicity on association football in Britain has been discussed in terms of its contribution to the development of civil society in Scotland and Northern Ireland. By highlighting the history of football clubs formed by the Irish in a major English city such as Liverpool this book seeks to broaden discussion out from the Scottish and Northern Irish scene it has hitherto exclusively been examined in. Primarily, we seek to explain why - in contrast to the historical development of similar ethno-religiously divided towns and cities in Scotland and Northern Ireland - football clubs emerging from the Irish community in Liverpool did not become a serious cultural force or attract a mass-based following.

Table of Contents

Introduction

One important cultural manifestation of the Irish Diaspora of the nineteenth century was the creation of sporting organisations based on ethno-religious lines. This was particularly the case in association football in Scotland and Northern Ireland where the Catholic Irish gave rise to their own football organisations. Clubs such as Derry Celtic, Belfast Celtic, Glasgow Celtic, Hibernian (Edinburgh), Dundee Harp and Dundee Hibernian (later to become Dundee United), played a key role in the maintenance of a distinct Gaelic-Irish identity. By contrast, in Liverpool - a city who's history and culture bears closer comparison with cities in Scotland and Northern Ireland than with other major English towns and cities - the Irish Catholic community did not establish and sustain an independent form of football representation.

The apparent absence of a specifically Irish dimension to football club development in Liverpool has led perplexed football historians to turn their discussion on the issue of ethnicity, religion and football in Liverpool to a debate concerning the possible divergent ethno-religious leanings of Everton and Liverpool football clubs – historically the city's largest professional football organisations - as a means of accommodating the city's religious schism in a sporting context. One of the purposes of this book is to allow a more complex picture to emerge of the Liverpool Irish response to football's development in their adopted city. To this end, evidence is presented which highlights the existence of a number of amateur Irish clubs overlooked in the chronicling of Liverpool's football history. This evidence demonstrates that, in point of fact, there *was* an ethnic Irish dimension to football club formation in

Liverpool and this discovery prompts an enquiry into why they failed to command the popularity enjoyed by similar ethnic Irish clubs in other parts of Britain: why, in other words, with such a huge potential support base to draw upon - in a locality where the social relations of ethnicity and religion loomed large - did Liverpool's Irish football clubs not emerge as a serious force within the game in that city? Another objective of this study, therefore, is to explore possible explanations for the retardation and demise of Liverpool's Irish football clubs. We do this by locating them within the prevailing socio-political context of the Irish Catholic experience in late nineteenth century Liverpool.

From the evidence gathered it is concluded that Liverpool Irish clubs may have been greatly weakened by the, at best, ambiguous attitude of the Irish religious and political hierarchy of the city toward the promotion of a distinctive Irish identity for the Catholic community. Our evidence further suggests that, unlike in Scotland and Northern Ireland, ethnicity and religion do not appear to have been hugely divisive issues in the development of football in Liverpool. During a period when they were deemed culturally marooned within Liverpool society, football provided a bridgehead between the Liverpool Irish and the host community. For these reasons the necessity for separate football represention was not an obvious requirment in Liverpool. In arguing this we acknowledge both the important social cleavage ethno-religious relations caused in Liverpool (the city's so called "exceptionalism" has been used by some writers to indicate Liverpool's distinctive socio-political terrain in comparison with other English towns and cities) but highlight a *simultaneous process* toward convergence in order to underline the point that community relations over the religious divide in Liverpool were more multi-layered and complex than simple sectarian hostitlity.

Liverpool's Irish Football Clubs

As can be seen from the census data in Table 1, proportionate to its population, Liverpool experienced mass migration from Ireland on a far greater scale than any other large English town or city in the nineteenth century.

Table 1   Proportion of Irish Born in the Populations of Major English Cities, 1871 & 1891 (nearest, 000)

1871	Irish Born	Total Population	Irish Born as % Of Total Pop	1891	Irish Born	Total Population	Irish Born as % Of Total Pop
Liverpool	76,000	493,000	15.4%	Liverpool	47,000	517,000	9.1%
Manchester	34,000	379,000	9%	Manchester	23,000	505,000	4.6%
Newcastle	7,000	119,000	5.9%	Newcastle	5,000	186,000	2.7%
Leeds	9,000	259,000	3.5%	Leeds	7,000	367,000	2%
London	91,000	3,453,000	2.6%	London	66,00	4,211,000	1.6%
Sheffield	6,000	240,000	2.5%	Sheffield	4,000	344,000	1.2%
B'ham	9,000	344,000	2.6%	B'ham	5,000	478,000	1%
Bristol	3,900	185,700	2.1%	Bristol	2,500	221,600	1.1%

Source: 1871 Census of England and Wales, vol.III, Population Abstracts: Birthplaces of the People; 1891 Census of England and Wales, vol.III, Population Abstracts: Birthplaces of the People.

Whilst it is worth making the point that not all of the 'Irish-born' in the census data can automatically be identified with Irish culture, beliefs and customs (for example, in Liverpool there was a colony of Ulster Protestant immigrants who were staunchly British in their social and political outlook) there was an undeniably large population in Liverpool in the second half of the nineteenth century who were distinct from the rest of Liverpool society by virtue of their religious and political culture. The Catholic Irish from the mid nineteenth century, in response to a largely hostile reception from the host community, developed in the dockside districts of north Liverpool what historian John Belchem has called an 'infrastructure of ethnic solidarity'. Organisations designed to meet the special needs – spiritual, economic and recreational – of every identifiable group within the Catholic population were established. Under the umbrella of the Catholic parish and the Irish Nationalist movement a distinctive Liverpool Irish community was sustained through insurance provision, orphanages, temperance societies and Irish cultural associations such as the Ancient Order of Hibernians and the Gaelic League. One cultural phenomenon previously overlooked by historians, however, was the formation of Liverpool Irish association football teams (see Table 2).

Table 2 Liverpool's Irish Football Clubs: 1880s/1890s

	Period in Existence	Standard of Play
Celtic	Sept. 1890 – April 1898	Liverpool & District Alliance League; Liverpool & District Amateur League
Celtic Rovers	Jan. 1891 – Sept. 1892	Non-League
Celtic Swifts	Sept. 1892 – Oct. 1893	Non-League
Eldonians	Sept. 1894 – Dec. 1894	Everton & District Alliance League
Liverpool Celtic	Jan. 1891 – March 1891	Non-League
Liverpool Hibernian	Oct. 1890 – Jan. 1891	Non-League
Old Xaverians	Sept. 1895 –	Lancashire I Zingari League
St. Anthony's	Sept. 1897 – April 1898	Non-League
St. Francis Xavier	Sept. 1888 – Nov. 1889	Non-League
St. Sylvester	Nov. 1888 – April 1896	Everton & District Junior League
5th Irish	Sept. 1888 – Nov. 1894	Liverpool & District Amateur League; Liverpool Senior League; West Lancashire League

Source: *Liverpool Daily Post, Liverpool Football Echo*

Just as in areas of mass Irish Catholic settlement in Scotland and Northern Ireland, a number of football clubs were formed in Liverpool. The formation of football clubs in Catholic parishes was part of a trend in Liverpool which had seen earlier forays into football by Protestant churches. In an earlier period, Church of England parishes and Nonconformist congregations pioneered the development of football in Liverpool (a partuicular manifestatation of the general advance of sport in Liverpool prompted by religious leaders concerned that the increase in leisure time of male workers in particular would be taken up by gambling and alcohol consumption). Indeed, the origins of four out of the five Merseyside clubs that played football professionally are to be found in such religious organisations: both Everton and Liverpool football clubs can trace their roots back to the St. Domingo New Connexional Methodist chapel team formed in 1878; Tranmere Rovers were formed by young men from the congregation of the Wesleyan Methodist chapel at Whitfield Street, Higher Tranmere in 1884; and Bootle FC, a Football League club during the early 1890s, evolved from the Bootle St. Johns Church of England amateur team established in 1879. Liverpool Caledonians Football Club, a club employing professionals and playing in the Lancashire League, were the exception to this rule, being formed by businessmen from the Liverpool Scottish merchant community in 1891. Even here, though, the shared Presbyterianism of many of the clubs major figures could be argued to have been a unifying force. From available evidence relating to the religious denomination of six of the seven club directors in 1892, three were Presbyterians. Evidence gained about shareholders also reveals a strong Presbyterian presence.

The earliest recorded information about a Catholic team being formed was that of Saint Francis Xavier Football Club, established in September 1888 in the Everton district of north Liverpool. The parish had been founded in the then fashionable Everton in 1848, and had a strong connection to Stoneyhurst Jesuit College in Lancashire where many of its clergy and prominent laymen were educated. Saint Francis Xavier's was, according to the parish historian, 'attended mainly by people who had the dual advantages of money and education'. In the provision of sport, the parish was in the forefront of Catholic efforts in Liverpool. The college attached to Saint Francis Xavier's church also established cricket and rugby teams. The setting up of the Old Xaverian's Athletic Association in 1898 – adding a tennis club, cycling club and harriers club for ex-pupils - was the first of its kind for a college or school in the area. In common with the setting up of sporting bodies by other churches, the Association's foundation seems to have been a measure taken, in part at least, to counter the threat of apostasy amongst young parishioners. Writing in 1899 in *The Xaverian* (the college journal), the Reverand Father Parry commented that there was 'a necessity for Catholic Associations in a large town like Liverpool as otherwise our Catholic young men would join non-Catholic associations'.

The first non-parish based Irish team: 5th Irish Football Club (known as 'The Irishmen' in local football circles), also dates from 1888, and it too was based in the district of Everton. The team's origins lay in the 5th Irish Volunteer Rifle Brigade, a body of men recruited exclusively from the Liverpool Irish Catholic community. The Catholic Church played a significant role in the life of the 'Irish Brigade': the chaplain of the Brigade was the celebrated Monsignor

James Nugent, a figure central to the charitable effort in the Irish districts of Liverpool in the late nineteenth century; whilst the Brigade and it's later manifestation – the 8th Irish Battalion – drew many of its officer recruits from Saint Francis Xavier college.

The remainder of the 1880s and early 1890s saw a spate of Irish teams being set up in north Liverpool - both parish and non-parish based. In addition to the Liverpool Irish football clubs that were formed, Irish immigrants in nearby Bootle produced two teams of their own: Bootle Hibernians and Bootle Celtic. The last decade of the nineteenth century, therefore, saw the Irish community well represented in local amateur football circles and their existence certainly demonstrates that the Liverpool Irish played a part in the development of football on Merseyside. However, to add perspective to this analysis, it must also be recognised that most of these clubs had a relatively short lived and inauspicious history. So fleeting was their existence that little record is left of them beyond the scorelines of their organised games and their secretary's appeal in the local press for fixtures. Certainly, none could claim to have been embraced by the local Irish community in the manner that some Irish clubs in Scotland and Northern Ireland had been during this same period. In Liverpool, only 5th Irish, Celtic and St. Sylvester's football clubs remained in existence beyond two seasons. Most of the Liverpool Irish clubs played in "general" matches (informal, non-league fixtures arranged between teams – usually from the same neighbourhood or district) with only 5th Irish and Celtic playing in organised local amateur leagues on anything like a regular basis. 5th Irish played for two years in the local Volunteer Brigade football league before entering the newly formed Liverpool and District Amateur League in 1890. They acquitted themselves creditably in the Liverpool and District league, claiming top three placings in two out of the three seasons they were involved in it. The club then switched to the West Lancashire and District League for season 1893/94, which turned out to be their last season in league competition. For their part Celtic played in the Liverpool and District Minor League and Liverpool and District Amateur League between 1891 and 1898, generally achieving mid-table respectability. By the end of the nineteenth century, though, attempts by the Liverpool Irish at creating independent football clubs had all but been abandoned. The formation of the Liverpool Catholic Schools Football League in 1900 (keeping 'football enthusiasts in a Catholic atmosphere') symbolised a more general retreat to within its own community for Irish football identity in the city. None of the wave of amateur clubs formed from their community during the 1880s and 1890s were nurtured into organisations of mass following capable of challenging the best of those of the host community, none transformed into professional clubs by the substantial strata of Liverpool Irish professionals and businesmen – a process common to the development of Irish clubs elsewhere in Britain.

What, then, can explain the retardation of the Liverpool Irish clubs? In the remainder of this study we argue that in Liverpool an ideological impetus for the establishment and development of a separate and distinct Irish football presence was deliberately withheld by the Liverpool Irish hierarchy. We also argue that another important factor in the retardation and demise of Liverpool Irish football clubs was the absence of any significant social barrier to Irish Catholic involvement in football clubs developed by the host community in that city. It is clear that in the case of Irish Catholic clubs in Scotland and Northern

Ireland those two structural factors proved to be key in nurturing the seeds of amateur Irish teams into professional organisations: a state of affairs that fostered a determination amongst minority Irish Catholic communities to create and sustain their own football clubs as symbols of their permanence.

The Attitude of Liverpool's Catholic and Irish Political Hierarchy Toward Irish Football Clubs

In Scotland and in Northern Ireland the Roman Catholic Church and Nationalist politicians were crucial to the establishment and early development of the football clubs that eventually gained mass support from the immigrant Catholic Irish. Hibernian (Edinburgh), Glasgow Celtic, Dundee Harp and Belfast Celtic all received their initial impetus from the Catholic Church. Hibernian were formed in 1875 by members of the St. Patrick's Catholic Young Men's Society (CYMS) in the Leith area of Edinburgh. The club was a prime source of income for the CYMS in its charitable activities. Glasgow Celtic were founded in similar circumstances, as a response to the challenge of providing relief to the poor in parishes in the East End of Glasgow. Many members of the Celtic committee were involved in the Society of St Vincent de Paul, a body of Catholic laymen who undertook work amongst the very poorest of the parish. Dundee Harp were another club founded by the members of a CYMS. The club's origins owed more than a small debt to Hibernian FC who's appearances in Dundee to aid the coffers of local Catholic charities inspired Harp's formation. Initially, then, these clubs performed an important practical role as generators of charitable relief for the Catholic community. But they were also viewed, along with other sports and pastimes, as a means to focus young Catholics toward leisure activities supervised by the church. The men behind the creation of Hibernians and Dundee Harp, in particular, were closely identified with the temperance movement, and Belfast Celtic's existence can be traced back to the church's encouragement of Catholic laymen to provide "responsible" leisure activities for Catholics in Belfast and Derry - objectives complimentary to the Catholic Church's attempts to staunch leakage of their natural constituency to evangelising Protestant sects operating within the urban environment.

The presence of Nationalist politicians in the early development of these clubs, though, indicates that they were also viewed as vehicles for the advancement of Irish Home Rule politics. The reach such sporting organisations had into communities, and their conspicuous adoption of an Irish or Gaelic cultural identity, perhaps making them an inevitable pole of attraction for Nationalist politicians. Club committee members of Hibernian were conspicuoulsy involved in the Edinburgh Home Rule movement during the 1880s and 1890s. Men like John McFadden and Michael Flanagan - members of the St Patrick's CYMS and also involved in the running of Hibernian Football Club - were outspoken in their commitment to Irish Home Rule. Due to their influence Hibernian FC was the base for two branches of the Irish National League in the Scottish capital, and the Edinburgh club became very much identified with the cause of Irish Home Rule. Though the connection between Home Rule politics and Glasgow Celtic Football Club may not have been as formally established as at Hibernian, Irish political figures provided the club with its organizational backbone. Club committeemen, William McKillop (a Nationalist MP for North Sligo), John Glass and Tom Colgan were involved in Irish nationalist politics in Glasgow via organisations such as the Young Ireland Society and the Irish National League. In Northern Ireland, Belfast Celtic were also strongly influenced by men for whom Nationalist politics was a driving force. The club's first chairman, Dan McCann, was a founder member of the

National Club in Belfast, the halls of which acted as headquarters for Belfast Celtic's club committee. Another man closely associated with the early period of the Belfast club was Joe Devlin, Nationalist MP for West Belfast. Devlin's rise to political prominence and Belfast Celtic's emergence as a mass supported club were mutually enhancing.

There seems little doubt that the strong religious and nationalist influence at these clubs was key their attraction of a mass following and establishment as serious forces within their football environment. At a later stage, driven on by competitive requirements to find substantial funding, it was their established cultural importance and mass support which attracted the attention and cash of businessmen capable of overseeing the incorporation of these members' clubs into football club companies. Some of these people were original club members (those involved in politics were often businessmen or well-to-do professionals), others were new to football, perhaps seeing in their association the possibility of vending rights to clubs (brewers and others in the drink trade were quick to purchase shares in Glasgow Celtic, Hibernian and Belfast Celtic). The possibility of utilising football to commercially exploit the tension of ethnic rivalries is said to have been a key motivation for involvement in share ownership of Glasgow's major football clubs. For others, though, the kudos of being closely connected to an ethno-cultural asset was viewed as an end in itself.

In comparison, the potential of Irish football clubs in Liverpool to fulfil the social and political roles (and, indeed, open the entreprenurial possibilities) that motivated the establshment of their sister clubs in Scotland and Northern Ireland appears to have been largely ignored by the city's Irish leadership. As we have already witnessed, the impulse to create football teams independent of the host population existed in Liverpool. However, there is little evidence to suggest that a concerted attempt was made to formally support and develop these clubs as competitive orgnaisations attracting mass support. Only for Saint Francis Xavier Football Club is there documentary evidence highlighting serious efforts to elevate a parish-based team to the level of organisation required to be competitive in local leagues. The Saint Francis Xavier club committee was presided over by a member of the clergy, Reverend Father Brown. The club committee also included well-to-do Catholic layman, William Sparrow, a barrister and the son of cotton manufacturer, John Sparrow. In 1888 the committee took steps to organise the club along the lines of a fee-paying membership, sending out an appeal for finances to cover the running costs of a football team. However, this project ended in failure and the club, despite an impressive playing record, was wound up less than a year later. Football club organisation did re-emerge at St Francis Xavier's in 1895 with the formation of Old Xaverian's Football Club whose teams were assembled from former students of the college. Old Xaverian's Football Club (formed in 1895) were, however, a staunchly amateur club. It appears that, though they were conspicuously successful in the Lancashire I Zingari League, they were disinterested in widening the appeal of the club by, for example, playing non-old boys of the college. As part of the wider St Francis Xavier Association, the existence of the Old Xaverian's seems primarily to have been to provide a Catholic professional class with an opportunity for fraternalism. This verse of the Association's song perhaps underlines the point:

Politics, art, money and mart bind men together, but not from the heart;

Sport is our bond, lovingly donned, light are the fetters of which we are fond,

Under His rule we, his votaries, find - vigour and health, both for body and mind.

There is no evidence either to suggest that – as with Nationalists in Scotland and Northern Ireland who embraced "the Garrison Game" - Nationalist in Liverpool were interested in forming and developing specifically Irish association football clubs in the city. It is perhaps to be expected that Nationalist politicians in Liverpool would have been opposed to any association with 5th Irish Football Club – the highest profile club formed to represent the Liverpool Irish. Due to their loyalty to British military objectives, Irish Nationalist attitude toward the Volunteer Brigade that the team was drawn from was far from fraternal. Though the Battalion was subject, on occasion, to attack from Orange mobs – thus marking it out as "of" the Liverpool Irish community – it was still a foreign body in Nationalist eyes. The Gaelic League in Liverpool, for example, berated the men of the 5th Irish Brigade who '…joined the volunteers in their thousands to resist a French invasion to evict the Saxon…', and posed the question: 'Can we [in this context] wonder that the English statesmen refuse to grant Ireland Home Rule?' However, Nationalists in Liverpool apparently felt no inclination to form or support any alternative football club to 5th Irish. This is not to suggest sports were viewed as uselss to the Nationalist cause. A variety of Nationalist-inspired sporting societies were formed in Liverpool in the last two decades of the nineteenth century such as Hurling clubs, Gaelic football clubs and a Celtic Cycling Club. However, the encouragement of Irish nationalists to establish interest in Gaelic games failed. As the chairman of the Lancashire Board of the Gaelic Athletic Association

(GAA) remarked in 1904 in relation to the paucity of Liverpool clubs and associations '…a greater measure of support than has hitherto been accorded by the large Irish population of the district' would be required. The sum total of the GAA presence in Liverpool at the end of the nineteenth century was just three hurling clubs: *Dibirtheacha O'Eirinn; Young Ireland; and Lamh Dearg.*

De-Nationalisation of the Liverpool Irish

The disinclination of the religious leaders of Irish Liverpool to lend their support to the formation of specifically Irish football clubs might be understood in the context of the ideological hostitlity of the Liverpool diocese towards the promotion and assertion of ethnic identity. The Church's policy in Liverpool was to incorporate the immigrant Irish and their descendents into British mainstream life by "denationalising" them of their Irishness whilst maintaining their commitment to

Catholicism. The city's Catholic hierarchy were determined to foster an air of respectability for Catholicism. Due to their general level of poverty and their perceived active or passive support for Irish Home Rule the immigrant Irish were viewed as a social and political threat to the native population and thereby a force that could thwart the ambition of Catholic rehabilitation. We have already seen in relation to Irish settlement in Liverpool that part of the strategy of the Catholic Church hierarchy toward the Irish was to construct a network of charitable organisations aimed at the physical and moral improvement of the Irish-born immigrant and their offspring. Another strategy that the Church adopted involved a concentrated attack on the nurturing of a distinct Irish culture, more especially one defining itself in opposition to British culture: loyalty to the state being a crucial element of respectability. This was to be achieved by a re-education policy for the Irish population focussing on and celebrating dominant British values. In schools emphasis was placed on religious instruction, whilst secular studies made little reference to Ireland or its people's affairs. This policy extended to the vetting of Irish priests who were preparing to serve in English parishes. Parish priests had a key role to play in overseeing the moral tone in a parish, and any indication that an Irish priest held opinions which might have had an Irish congregation being aroused to political fervour would have resulted in that priest failing to gain a placement in England. This policy is almost cdertain to have impacted on the make up of the clergy in Liverpool. During the whole of the second half of the nineteenth century - a period in which, as we have seen, Liverpool experienced mass Irish migration and the demographic profile of the Church in Liverpool was transformed overwhelmingly into an Irish Catholic one - the Roman Catholic Diocese of Liverpool employed just 90 priests born and ordained in Ireland. The vast majority of priests serving in Liverpool during this period (301 out of 391) were either born and ordained in England (more usually in Lancashire) or else were foreign-born missionaries.

In Liverpool, the English Catholic hierarchy had proven itself to be particularly outspoken against the Irish nationalist cause. Bishop Goss (Catholic Bishop of Liverpool between 1856 and1872) was a stern critic of the Fenianism which had gained a foothold in Liverpool and believed that the Irish would only come to be accepted in Liverpool society if they played down their ethnicity. Bishop (later Archbishop) Whiteside (the leader of Liverpool's Roman Catholic church between 1894 and 1921) was openly Unionist in his politics and often crossed swords with the Liverpool Irish National League. Under the leadership of Bishops Goss and Whiteside the appointemnt of continental clerical orders to Irish districts was a feature of recruitment in the Archdiocese. Benedictine, Franciscan and Jesuit orders ministered to many of the parishes of Irish Liverpool. In the Vauxhall district, for example, Benedictine monks ran St.

Mary's and St. Peter's parishes; in Everton district St. Mary of the Angels was a Franciscan run parish, and Jesuits ministered at St. Francis Xavier's. St. Anthony's parish Scotland Road (the largest parish in Irish Liverpool) was founded by French missionary priests and became known locally as the "French Church". Only at Holy Cross in Vauxhall - which was under the jurisdiction of an Irish missionary order: the Oblates of Mary Immaculate - was a distinctively Irish identity reinforced and celebrated. The parish lay outside the jurisdiction of the Liverpool Roman Catholic Diocese and it is instructive that here at least their was clerical organisation of specifically 'Celtic' societies for their parishioners. The continental clerical orders which carried out the Church's teachings and work in much of Irish Liverpool were part of an "ultramontane" movement within the Catholic Church (ultramontane meaning, literally, 'beyond the mountain' – that is, the Vatican City's location beyond the Alps) which stressed a commitment to papal authority over and above any of the local pre-occupations that the Church or its constituency in any individual country may have had. In common with the wishes of the English hierarchy these Catholic orders were part of an enterprise whose ultimate aim was the incorporation and denationalisation of Irish Catholics.

One effect of the church's denationalisation strategy in Liverpool seems to have been the creation of distinct parochial identities, something which would have played an important part in negating, or at least de-emphasising, any overarching (and unifying) Irish identity amongst the Liverpool Irish. Interestingly, competition between parishes in sports was especially encouraged: boxing, swimming and particularly football rivalries were fierce. The Catholic Schools Cup and Catholic Schools Shield competitions are said to have engendered 'intense' competition between parishes in the Irish districts of the city. Rather than helping to unite the Liverpool Irish around a common ethno-religious identity, sport in the parochial system (in conjunction with varying levels of poverty and quality of housing between parishes) appears to have been utilised to stratify and reinforce division through the establishment of micro-cultures. That stratification, it can be said, acted as a bulwark against the creation of, and a coalescing around, ethno-religious totems – say, for example, a professional football club - capbable of attracting the support of all of Irish Liverpool behind it. Certainly, given the Catholic Church's endeavours in Liverpool to ensure that the "Irishness" of its congregation was minimized, it seems reasonable to assert that encouragement to set up or support ethno-religious sporting organisations capable of mobilising ethnic sentiments would have run counter to its own de-nationalising strategy.

When assessing the failure of an ideological lead for a Liverpool Irish football club to emerge we must also consider the changing objectives and priorities of local Nationalist politicians. It has been established by football historians that the involvement of local political figures in the foundation and control of football clubs in Britain – at Irish and non-Irish clubs alike – was substantial. The popularity of the game amongst the urban working class made it almost inevitable that politicians would attempt to associate themselves with the game. Identification in one form or another with the town's professional football club would have been a priority for local men holding political ambitions. Nowhere more was this the case than in Liverpool, where Liberal and Conservative politicians became closely associated with the professional clubs of the city. By contrast, and as we have seen, the Liverpool Irish political community appear to have had no interest in forming or supporting the development of an Irish alternative to the professional clubs of the host community as Nationalists had done elsewhere. Again, this state of affairs may have been influenced by local factors. The Nationalist movement in Liverpool by the end of the nineteenth century had evolved into one concerned more with the material conditions endured by the working class Liverpool Irish in their dockside communities than with the affairs of Irish nationhood. Irish Nationalists in Liverpool had by this point – and on the basis of franchise reforms that gave many more of the working class a means of constitutional expression – usurped the Liberal Party in electoral terms in Irish Liverpool, replacing them in the city as the primary political organisation representing Irish interets. Though still committed to Irish Home Rule this work was increasingly being subordinated to a class-based approach to Irish affairs. Over the last two decades of the nineteenth century, as Nationalists gained a firm foothold in municipal politics in Liverpool, aspirations for an independent Ireland began to give way to pragmatism: to serve their dockland constituency in terms of securing better housing and sanitary conditions. By the century's end social reformers such as John O'Shea and the Harford brothers, Austin and Frank - who enjoyed influence over the dockland council wards - had wrested control of the local Irish Party away from traditional Home Rule Nationalists like Alderman J.G. Lynskey – men whose counsel to his colleagues was to remember they were Irishman first, and Liverpudlians after. The Liverpool movement's continued link with the struggle for an independent Ireland was manifest through their work to return to parliament Thomas Power O'Connor, the Irish Nationalist MP for the Liverpool Scotland constituency. However, relations were strained between local activists and O'Connor. O'Connor, an Irish journalist, was viewed as an outsider thrust upon the local movement by the Irish parliamentary leadership and as someone with little interest in the everyday existence of the Liverpool Irish community he represented. The Liverpool organisation was by this time, in all but name, a Catholic labour party, intent on delivering the type of municipal reforms in terms of housing, health and employment that the local Tory leadership were delivering on behalf of local Protestant workers who formed the base of their electoral support in Liverpool. The Nationalist leadership, then, were becoming increasingly ambivalent about pressing the ethnic profile of their constituency over and above their class position – hardly a conducive environment to sustain a football club with a strong Irish identity.

Integration of the Liverpool Irish and Merseyside's Football Environment

The absence of an ideological impetus to set up Irish football clubs was compounded by the accommodation of the immigrant Irish within the Merseyside football environment. In terms of professional football the evidence underlines that strong links were forged between both Everton and Liverpool football clubs and the Irish community – links which stretched from the boardroom to the terraces. At Everton Football Club this was especially the case. From its inception, some of the club's most influential committee members (and boardroom directors after Everton incorporated in 1892) were also supporters of the Liverpool Home Rule movement. Irishman, Dr William Whitford, a surgeon, was the chairman of the Everton Liberal Party district association and an ardent Home Ruler. In an impassioned speech during the municipal election campaign of 1892 Whitford railed against the blocking of Home Rule by Ulster Unionists:

> Ulstermen do not desire to govern Ireland according to the wishes of the people of Ireland, but according to the narrow prejudices of the so-called 'loyal minority'. Irish Catholic bishops and priests had not the illegitimate power we in this country are asked to believe. Their views are, however, in accordance with the nationalist aspirations of the Irish people. The priests had been loyal to the people, unlike the priests of other denominations...The Irish priests could not and had not the power to lead the Irish people in temporal matters against their honest convictions.

Director and later chairman of Everton, James Clement Baxter, was a prominent Catholic layman and Liberal city councillor for the predominantly Irish St. Anne's Ward (or, as the *Liverpool Catholic Herald* described him: 'the Catholic and Home Rule' representative for that ward). Like Whitford, Baxter was a surgeon, though with 'considerable financial concerns in cinema interests', and was a key financial figure in Everton's early history having guaranteed the club's commitment to move grounds from Anfield to Goodison Park in 1892. Baxter's son, Cecil Stuart Baxter, followed in his footsteps into the club boardroom, and also like his father becoming Everton chairmen. Another Everton director and fellow Liberal-Nationalist of Whitford and Baxter, Alderman Alfred Gates (a name which was 'as a red rag to a furious bull' to the Conservative-Unionist Party, according to the *Liverpool Daily Post* in 1910) was a 'strenuous advocate of Home Rule' keen to show that 'the Orange Tory Party were losing ground in Liverpool'. And Everton's first chairman, Dublin educated George Mahon, helped reorganise the Walton Liberal Association in the wake of the defection of Liberal Unionists opposed to Gladstone's proposed solution to the Irish Question. Mahon was a prime mover in the Walton Liberal Association's adoption of the Home Rule policy and was one of the officers of that district body affirming in the local press their 'total support for Home Rule'.

At Liverpool FC there were also opportunities for those of the Irish Catholic community (or those sympathetic toward it) seeking controlling roles – though only after a fashion. It is likely that there would have been some opposition to Irish Catholic involvement at boardroom level during its formative period under the leadership of John Houlding, the club's founder and majority shareholder. Houlding's earlier role in local football as honorary president and principal financial sponsor of Everton FC was instrumental in that club's rise to national prominence and success during the 1880s and early 1890s. A complex dispute over the control of Everton between Houlding and those opposing him on the club committee – in large part politically motivated - led to him setting up the rival Liverpool FC to occupy Everton's vacated Anfield ground in 1892. Houlding, a brewer, was a Conservative city councillor and a staunch Unionist. He tended to recruit to his Liverpool FC boardroom men who shared his social and political outlook. Perhaps the most significant of connections existing between members of the Liverpool hierarchy were those forged through involvement in the Working Men's Conservative Association (WMCA). The Liverpool WMCA had established itself as the dominant force in Liverpool politics. The engine of Protestant power within the Conservative Party, the organisation kept Liverpool Conservatism at the vanguard of anti-Catholic, and so-called anti-Ritualist, opposition at a time when independent Protestant representation threatened the Tory's "natural" majority in the council chamber. Apart from Houlding, other members of the earliest Liverpool FC boards involved in the WMCA were directors Benjamin E. Bailey, Edwin Berry, Albert Edward Berry, Richard Webster, William Houlding, and club secretary, Simon Jude. Masonic involvement amongst directors at Liverpool FC was also an interconnecting factor. John Houlding, a founding member of both Anfield and Sir Walter Raleigh Lodges, rose through the levels of Freemasonry, attaining the status of Provincial Grand Registrar, and Provincial Grand Warden in West Lancashire during the 1880s. His Masonic career reached its zenith in 1898 when becoming Grand Senior Deacon of England. The majority of directors at the club whilst he was in control of the club were also Freemasons.

At boardroom level, then, the early period of Liverpool FC's history –
the 'Houlding' period – does seem to be defined by a pronounced Tory Party-
Masonic-Protestant profile. In the context of sectarian tensions in Liverpool
society at this juncture this does lends some weight to the often-made claims
concerning a historical sectarian division between Everton and Liverpool
football clubs. However, after Houlding's death in 1902 and the restructuring of
the club in the years following - including a vast growth in share ownership –
any obstacle that may have been placed in the path of Catholics being appointed
to senior positions in that club seem to have been removed. Three Catholics:
publicans, John Joseph Hill and Thomas Crompton (a former Everton player),
and timber merchant (and Old Xaverian FC player), William Harvey Webb,
joined the Liverpool board in the years following John Houlding's death.

Census records relating to shareholders of Everton and Liverpool in
1892 – the year of their formation as limited companies - also demonstrates that
the Irish-born had an ownership presence. Though, proportionate to their
presence in the city, they do not appear to have taken up as many football club
shares as other prominent immigrant groups in Liverpool such as the Scots and
Welsh, their investment indicates that there was no barrier for those financially
able to do so in the Irish community to hold a stake in the host society's
principal football clubs. Two of the most well known men in the Liverpool
Irish political community were shareholders at Everton and Liverpool:
Nationalist councillor for Vauxhall ward, John Gregory Taggart, was a
shareholder in Everton FC, and the aforementioned Austin Harford, Nationalist
councillor for the South Scotland ward (later to become Lord Mayor of
Liverpool) and chairman of the Old Xaverian Football Club, held shares in

Liverpool FC. Moreover, the association with Everton and Liverpool football clubs of Nationalist political figures and businessmen points to the probabilty that many more people within Irish Liverpool had also established a connection with them. Anecdotal evidence does suggest that the Liverpool Irish community contributed significantly to the support of the city's professional clubs on the terraces in this early period after incorporation. With Everton, especially, there appears to have been a strong association. According to Reverand James Handley, the first historian of Celtic Football Club '…Everton Football Club, like Celtic, owed its success to immigrant support, the Irish in Liverpool rallying wholeheartedly round it'. This view: that Everton were a club attracting strong Liverpool Irish support, is a recurrently expressed one in anecdotal accounts touching on the city's socio-cultural history.

This close relationship with both Everton and Liverpool would, perhaps, have partly been the result of Irish-born and second generation Irishmen becoming players at both Everton and Liverpool football clubs from a very early period in their history thus igniting ethnic pride in, and generating affection and support for, the host society's professional clubs. Everton had established a frequent supply line in Irish talent even prior to the twentieth century. Their first signing from Ireland was Jack Kirwan, a player plucked from Gaelic Football outfit St James Gaels in 1898. Kirwan's move to Goodison was followed by Shelbourne FC team mates Valentine Harris (another convert from Gaelic Football) and Billy Lacey. Many more were to follow as the club forged a connection so rich as to be described by Merseysdide football historian, Percy Young, as an 'Eireann tradition'. Whilst the earliest Liverpool FC teams included many players transferred from Scots-

Irish clubs who were of Irish Catholic descent, such as Andy McGuigan from Hibernian, and James McBride and Joseph McQue from Glasgow Celtic. Such identification with and loyalty toward Everton and Liverpool football clubs would obviously have affected the potential for the development of independent football expression to emerge from within the Liverpool Irish community.

This situation was very different to the football scene in Scotland and in Northern Ireland where the setting up of football clubs to cater to the Catholic Irish was a necessity if they were to participate in football on any level. Football in Scotland, due to deep underlying structural reasons, betrayed a strong anti-Catholic culture. Scottish cultural historian, Gerry Finn, argues that Scotland as a stateless nation in political and economic union with a dominant English partner largely fell back upon its dominant Presbyterian form of Protestantism to define "Scottishness". As such, Irish Catholics were viewed as the 'negative embodiment' of what it was to be Scottish, and the avenue into mainstream society appears to have been cut off. In this context football became an important arena for the refining of the notion of national identity – both Scottish and Irish – and the Scottish game became infected with anti-Catholic and anti-Irish prejudices because of it. Some football clubs in Scotland were closely identified with the Unionist cause, and the decision to exclude Catholic's from employment was an issue for Glasgow Rangers Football Club, in particular. At Rangers, the start of the twentieth century ushered in an era of vetting of new players and staff along religious lines and for existing Catholic employees to be asked to leave the club. Besides Rangers, clubs such as 3rd Edinburgh Rifle Volunteers, Larkhall Royal Albert and Clydebank also had Unionist and anti-Catholic reputations. The inability due to discriminatory practices in the host community of young Catholic Irishman in Edinburgh to find a football club to play for was a contributory reason for the establishment of Hibernian FC. This was also the case in Northern Ireland. Football clubs set up by Protestants dominated the game there. The most successful Northern Irish club, Belfast's Linfield FC, were (and remain) a football club strongly identified as a Protestant club for Protestants. In its earliest period, football in Northern Ireland was viewed by the majority community as being the preserve of people identifying themselves with the Union. As such, football helped to underscore the divisions between Unionists and Nationalist communities as clubs such as Belfast Celtic and Derry Celtic were formed to represent an excluded Irish Catholic population.

The obstructions Scottish and Northern Irish Catholic's faced in establishing their presence on the football scene gave an important impetus to the project of forming their own football organisations. Moreover, once formed, the opposition their clubs faced from the football establishment strengthened the resolve of the Irish Catholic community to sustain them. Scottish and Northern Irish Catholic clubs suffered physical attacks on their players, supporters and stadia. For example, the early history of Hibernian FC was marked by violence as anti-Irish mobs obstructed their use of pitches on common parkland. The Edinburgh club had to resort to forming its own guard in order to secure a playing area. In the west of Scotland, St. Peter's Football Club (a club established from the merger of Paisley Hibernians and Paisley Celtic) had its ground damaged on a regular basis, and the fixtures of Glasgow Celtic were often marked by crowd disturbances. In Northern Ireland, violence was a common occurrence against clubs associated with the Nationalist community, such as Belfast Celtic and Distillery, and later in the twentieth century against Derry City and Cliftonville. The history of Belfast Celtic, in particular, was, plagued by inter-communal violence and strife. Matches against teams with a pronounced Protestant identity like Linfield or Glentoran were used to launch ethno-religious tribal violence. Eventually, such violence took its toll: Belfast Celtic, having dropped out of the Irish League because of sectarian tensions between 1915 and 1918, and again between 1920 and 1924, were finally forced out of existence in 1949 amidst deteriorating conditions of safety for the club's staff and support. It has also been claimed that clubs from Irish Catholic communities in Scotland and Northern Ireland had also to contend with hostility from the football authorities. Initially, some of these clubs found it difficult to gain entry into their local and national leagues. The belief was strongly held that the Irish clubs were subject to biased decisions from the various football associations they were affiliated to when involved in disputes with so called 'native' clubs. Whether these concerns were real or imagined, there was a conviction amongst those who administered and supported Irish Catholic clubs that they were being victimised because of their association with religious and political beliefs alien to those controlling football in Scotland and Ireland.

By contrast, evidence relating to the treatment of Liverpool's Irish football clubs reveals no obvious examples of hostility to their presence on the local football scene. Liverpool Irish clubs capable of a competitive standard of play were invited to form part of the local leagues, and it appears that cordial relations existed between the Irish clubs and those of the host population. The Everton FC Committee, for example, on hearing of the neglect of the Liverpool Volunteer League to cast a trophy and present it to 5th Irish FC in recognition of their winning the Volunteers Football League Championship in 1890, provided and presented a commemorative shield of their own to 'the Irishmen'. Both Everton and Liverpool football clubs provided assistance to Saint Francis Xavier's Football Club by providing players to train their team in the 1890s. Everton player and future club director, Daniel Kirkwood, and Liverpool player, Alex McCowie, each spent time at Saint Francis Xavier's as team trainers. Other evidence suggests that their was free movement of players between Irish and non-Irish clubs. In 1888 the *Liverpool Football Echo* reported that Saint Francis Xavier players had joined local rivals Brittanic FC and, in turn, Brittanic players had joined the Catholic club. And the local football press gave the Irish clubs sympathetic coverage. 5th Irish match reports were given prominence in the *Liverpool Football Echo,* and the local press appear generally to have been encouraging toward other Liverpool Irish clubs.

It could be argued that this benign reaction was because, unlike in Scotland and Ulster, none of the Liverpool Irish clubs were in a position to challenge the superiority of the largest of the "native" clubs. Clearly, given the potential for sectarian violence in Liverpool during this period, it would be unrealistic to deny the credibility of this argument. However, as the historical development of Scottish football reveals, Irish-Scots clubs were faced by a hostile reaction to their presence prior to their elevation to any status as significant challengers to the most successful clubs of the host population. Overall, it can be said that the greatest difficulty facing Liverpool's Irish football clubs was in attracting the financial and moral support of the Liverpool Irish community itself, rather than any native animosity toward them. 5th Irish FC, for example, were forced to withdraw from league football due to an inability to pay for the ground its team played on. And evidence suggests that those behind the Saint Francis Xavier FC were critical of the level of support that was forthcoming for their team.

Epilogue

This study suggests that while the development of football in Liverpool did, to some extent, provide evidence of the Irish Catholic community's attempts to create a football club with a specifically ethno-religious identity, the Church and political hierarchy in Irish Liverpool were engaged in strategies that tended to eschew harnessing football as a major form of cultural capital. The Liverpool Catholic Church was more concerned with educating its Irish Catholic community with British values and norms in order to foster respectability for the Church. The limited development of Irish football organisation in the city can be said to have assisted this objective by ensuring that Catholicism was not so synonymous with Irish-Catholicism that it would adversely affect its capacity to cut across Irish-British identities, in accordance with its main aim of integration. For their part, the Irish political elite in Liverpool had a number of competing strategies which included Home Rule but that broader class based objectives of social reform had become, or were in the process of becoming, dominant. Nationalists in Liverpool represented a distinct ethnic group, but they were also compelled to struggle for the rights of social and political citizenship – manifest in their commitment to municipal politics. This led to eclecticism in the way in which the local Irish elite approached forms of cultural capital such as sport. On the one hand, the development of Gaelic games was encouraged by some within the religious and political hierarchy. On the other hand, Irish Nationalists proved to be just as much at home supporting and indeed actively developing British (or "garrison") sports.

Most notably this included their involvement in the two mainstream football clubs, Everton and Liverpool, whose appeal spanned the ethno-religious divide. By contrast, in Scotland and Northern Ireland it appears that ethnicity provided the crucial medium through which the Irish religious and political elite – in the face of the hostility of the forces of Protestant Unionism – exerted itself within localities. This context proved to be fertile ground for the development of separate Irish football organisations which acted as a form of cultural capital amenable to mediating, and so consolidating, the fluid boundaries between religion, ethnicity and politics whilst at the same time buttressing the defence against Protestant Unionism. Moreover, a British identity defined by Protestant Unionism and implacably opposed to Irish Home Rule provided the basis for a deepening hostility towards the presence of, and increasing acts of violence against, Irish football clubs. This, in turn, acted as a major spur to the development of separate Irish-Scots football organisations.

There is no doubting that the Liverpool Irish experienced hostility from their host community, or that many of them suffered social marginalisation and economic inequalities. The initial reaction against this was to erect (to use John Belchem's description again) an infrastructure of ethnic solidarity. However, there was a weakening of national identity amongst the immigrant Irish community in Liverpool toward the end of the nineteenth century - a decline in a sense of Irish brotherhood marked by declining attendances amongst Liverpool Irish societies. This downgrading of ethnic identity in Liverpool would have been affected by the de-naionalisation policy of the Liverpool Catholic Church and by the Nationalist's shift in emphasis toward class politics. On this basis, by the end of the nineteenth century the Liverpool Irish had begun the process of privatising their ethnicity. Outside of key symbolic dates in the calendar, such as celebrating St. Patrick's Day or reacting to Orange Day parades on July 12th they were increasingly less likely to formally demonstrate their ethnic distinctiveness in the manner in which large Irish Catholic communities in the towns and cities of Scotland and Northern Ireland continued to do. This was a trend accelerated by a growing sense of identification amongst the Liverpool Irish with their host society. During the Boer War, for example, Liverpool's premier parish organ, *The Xaverian,* was very open in its support for the British military campaign in South Africa. The journal carried regular articles by parishioners serving in the army there. In a speech to the Old Xaverian's Association, the chairman of that body expressed that their members 'wished to be good citizens of the Empire in which they lived'. This is not to suggest a uniformity of opinion in the Irish community on the issue of the Boer War. Many of the Irish Nationalists took a decidedly pro-Boer stance. One such Nationalist was councillor John G. Taggart (co-incidentally an Everton shareholder). Taggart declared on the occasion of a British military reversal that he 'rejoiced at England's misfortune because she is responsible for all of ours'. However, Taggart was far from representative of even other Liverpool Nationalists on this issue, much less all of Liverpool's Irish Catholics. Under these changing circumstances the interaction of immigrant and host community in the realm of football club formation and support would have been a completely understandable development. Though some in the Liverpool Irish community did continue to form their own ethno-religious football organisations, there was no groundswell of support for them or a belief that they and they alone could satisfy the passion of the immigrant Irish for football in Liverpool.

Bibliography

Anon. *The Liverpool Irishman: Or Annals of the Irish Colony in Liverpool.* Liverpool: J. King, 1906.

Ayres, Pat. *The Liverpool Docklands: Life and Work in Athol Street.* Liverpool: Dockland History Project, 1999.

Baxter, R. 'The Liverpool Labour Party, 1918-1963', (D.Phil. thesis, University of Oxford, 1969).

Belchem, John. *Merseypride: Essays in Liverpool Exceptionalism.* Liverpool: Liverpool University Press, 2000.

Belchem, John*The Liverpool Irish.* Liverpool: Liverpool University Press 2007.

Bennet, Canon. *Father Nugent of Liverpool.* St. Helens: Wood, Westworth and Co., 1949.

Boyce, Frank. 'From Victorian 'Little Ireland' to Heritage Trail: Catholicism, Community and Change in Liverpool's Docklands', in Swift and Gilley, *The Irish in Victorian Britain,*

Brady, Lawrence W. *T.P. O'Connor and the Liverpool Irish.* London: Royal Historical Society, 1983.

Bradley, J.M. 'Integration or Assimilation? Scottish Society, Football and Irish Immigrants', *IJHS,* vol.13, no.2: 61-79.

Boyle, Raymond. 'Football and Cultural Identity in Glasgow and Liverpool' (PhD thesis, University of Stirling, 1995).

Bradley, J.M. *Sport, Culture, Politics and Scottish Society: Irish Immigrants and the Gaelic Athletic Association.* Edinburgh: John Donald, 1998.

Burke, Thomas. *Catholic History of Liverpool.* Liverpool: Tinling, 1910.

Clegg, Barbara. *The Man Who Made Littlewoods: The Story of John Moores.* London: Hodder and Stoughton, 1993.

Cooke, Terry. *Scotland Road: The Old Neighbourhood.* Wirral: Birkenhead Press, 1987.

Coyle, Padraig. *Paradise Lost and Found: The Story of Belfast Celtic.* Edinburgh: Mainstream, 1999.

Cronin, Michael. *Sport and Nationalism in Ireland: Gaelic Games, Soccer and Irish Identity Since 1884.* Dublin: Four Courts Press, 1999.

Davies, Sam. *Liverpool Labour: Social and Political Influences on the Development of the Labour Party in Liverpool, 1900-1939.* Keele: Keele University Press, 1996.

Day, R. 'The Motivations of Some Football Club Directors: An Aspect of the Social History of Association Football, 1890-1914' (M.A. Dissertation, University of Warwick, 1976).

Donnelly, Margaret. *My Parish, Holy Cross.* Liverpool: Starfish Multi-Media, 2006.

Edge, Alan. *Faith of Our Fathers: Football as a Religion.* London: Two Heads, 1997.

Engman, M (ed), *Ethic Identity in Urban Europe.* Dartmouth: New York University Press, 1992.

Everton FC Bulk Shareholders File, Company no. BT 31/ 36624, Companies House, Cardiff.

Finn, Gerry P.T. 'Racism, Religion and Social Prejudice: Irish Catholic Clubs, Soccer and Scottish Society – I The Historical Roots of Prejudice' *IJHS* , vol.8, no. 1 (1991): 70-91.

Finn, Gerry P.T. 'Racism, Religion and Social Prejudice: Irish Catholic Clubs, Soccer and Society – II Social Identities and Conspiracy Theories', *International Journal of the History of Sport,* vol.8, no.3 (1991): 370-97.

Finn, Gerry P.T. 'Sporting Symbols, Sporting identities: Soccer and Inter-group Conflict in Scotland and Northern Ireland' in *Scotland and Ulster.* Edinburgh: Mercat Press,1994.

Finn, Gerry P.T. 'Faith, Hope and Bigotry', in G. Jarvie and G. Walker (eds), *Scottish Sport in the Making of the Nation: Ninety Minute Patriots?.* Leicester: Leicester University Press, 1994.

Finn, Gerry P.T. 'Scottish Myopia and Global Prejudices', in G.P.T. Finn and R. Giulianotti (eds), *Football Culture: Local Contests, Global Visions.* London: Frank Cass, 2000.

Fishwick, Nick. *English Football and Society, 1910-1950.* Manchester: Manchester University Press, 1989.

Forde, F. 'The Liverpool Irish Volunteers', *The Irish Sword*, vol.10, no.39, 106-23

Gallagher, Tom. 'A Tale of Two Cities: Communal Strife in Glasgow and Liverpool Before 1914', in Swift and Gilley, *The Irish in Victorian Britain.*

Handley, James E. *The Celtic Story: A History of the Celtic Football Club.* London: Stanley Paul, 1960.

Jackson, Dan. 'Friends of the Union: Liverpool, Ulster, and Home Rule, 1910-1914', *Transactions of the Historical Society of Lancashire and Cheshire,* number152, 2003.

Hickman, Mary J. *Religion, Class and Identity: The State, the Catholic Church and the Education of the Irish in Britain.* Aldershot: Avebury, 1995.

Kennedy, David. 'The Split of Everton FC, 1892: The Creation of Distinct Patterns of Boardroom Formation at Everton and Liverpool Football Clubs', *Sport in History,* vol. 23, no. 1 (2003):1-26

Kennedy, David. 'Class, Ethnicity and Civic Governance: A Social profile of Football Club Directors on Merseyside in the Late Nineteenth Century', *International Journal of the History of Sport,* vol..22, no.5 (2005): 845-49.

Kennedy, David., and Collins, Mike. 'Community Politics in Liverpool and the Governance of Professional Football in the Late Nineteenth Century', *Historical Journal,* vol.49, no.3 (2006): 761-88.

Kennedy, John. *St. Francis Xavier's, Liverpool, 1848-1998.* Liverpool: CBM Advertising, 1998.

Klapas, J.A. 'Geographical Aspects of Religious Change in Victorian Liverpool, 1837-1901', (MA thesis, University of Liverpool, 1977).

Lane, Tony. *Liverpool: City of the Sea.* Liverpool: Liverpool University Press, 1997

Liverpool FC Bulk Shareholders File, Company no. BT 31/35668, Companies House, Cardiff.

Lugton, Alan. *The Making of Hibernian.* Edinburgh: John Donald Publishers, 1999.

Mason, Tony. 'The Blues and the Reds', *Transactions of the Historical Society of Lancashire and Cheshire,* Vol. 134, 1985.

Murray, Bill. *The Old Firm: Sectarianism, Sport and Society in Scotland.* Edinburgh: John Donald Publishers, revised edition 2000.

Neal, F. *Sectarian Violence: The Liverpool Experience, 1819-1914.* Manchester: Manchester University Press, 1988.

Owen, Mike. *Everton in Europe, 1962-2005: Der Ball Ist Rund*. London: Countyvise, 2005.

Papworth, J.D. 'The Irish in Liverpool, 1835-1871: Segregation and Dispersal' (Ph.D thesis, University of Liverpool, 1981).

Plumb, Brian. *Found Worthy: A Biographical Dictionary of the secular Clergy of the Archdiocese of Liverpool (deceased) Since 1850*. Liverpool: Brian Plumb,1986.

Pooley, Colin. 'The Irish in Liverpool circa 1850-1940', in Engman, M (ed), *Ethic Identity in Urban Europe*. Dartmouth: New York University Press, 1992.

Rees, R. 'The Development of Physical Recreation in Liverpool During the Nineteenth Century', (MA thesis, University of Liverpool, 1968).

Roberts, D.A. 'Religion and Politics in Liverpool Since 1900', (M.sc. thesis, University of London, 1965).

Ross, Ian. and Smailes, Gordon. *Everton: A Complete Record*. Derby: Breedon Books, 1988.

Russell, Dave. *Football and the English*. Preston: Carnegie, 1997.

O'Connell, Bernard. 'The Irish Nationalist Party in Liverpool, 1873-1922' (MA thesis, University of Liverpool, 1971).

Sayle, Alexie *Barcelona Plates*. London: Hodder and Stoughton, 2000.

Smith, Tommy. *I Did it the Hard Way*. London: Arthur Baker, 1980.

Young, Percy M. *Football on Merseyside*. London: Stanley Paul, 1963.

Waller, Philip J. *Democracy and Sectarianism: A Political and Social History of Liverpool, 1868-1939*. Liverpool: Liverpool University Press, 1981.

Walvin, James. *The People's Game*. Edinburgh: Mainstream, 1994.

Williams, John. 'Out of the Blue and Into the Red: The Early Liverpool Years', in J. Williams (et al) *Passing Rhythms: Liverpool FC and the Transformation of Football*. Manchester: Berg, 2002.

Williams, John. *Into the Red: Liverpool FC and the Changing Face of English Football*. Edinburgh: Mainstream, 2001.

Woods, J. *Growin' Up: One Scouser's Social History of Liverpool* (Preston: Carnegie Press, 2004 second edition.

Printed in Poland
by Amazon Fulfillment
Poland Sp. z o.o., Wrocław